BRITAIN IN OLD PHOTOGRAPHS

EAST HAM

STEPHEN PEWSEY

SUTTON PUBLISHING LIMITED

Sutton Publishing Limited
Phoenix Mill · Thrupp · Stroud
Gloucestershire · GL5 2BU

First published 1996

Copyright © Stephen Pewsey, 1996

British Library Cataloguing in Publication Data
A catalogue record for this book is available from the
British Library.

ISBN 0-7509-1122-0

Typeset in 10/12 Perpetua.
Typesetting and origination by
Sutton Publishing Limited.
Printed in Great Britain by
Ebenezer Baylis, Worcester.

Front cover photograph: German Butcher's Shop, 1911. Herr Goetz was one of thousands of Germans who came to East Ham in the late nineteenth century in search of work and improved circumstances. His shop, which stood on the corner of High Street and Harrow Road, was recently demolished as part of the Ron Leighton Way road scheme. Flags flutter from lamp posts marking the coronation of George V, but within a few years most Germans and people with German-sounding names had to change their names after anti-German riots during the First World War.
Back cover photograph: construction work at Beckton Gasworks.

CONTENTS

ACKNOWLEDGEMENTS

I would like to thank all the members of Newham History Society, which celebrated its Silver Jubilee in 1996, for all the encouragement received over the years.

I am grateful to the London Borough of Newham for permission to reproduce some of the images used in this volume.

Thanks are also due to Miss Lilian Cameron for permission to reproduce the photograph of the Reid family.

All other pictures are from the author's own postcard collection or reproduced by permission of the Eclipse Archive. Special thanks go to Mark.

I also record my gratitude to my wife, Paulette, for all her technical assistance.

St Mary Magdalene, East Ham parish church; a fine example of Norman architecture.

INTRODUCTION

For centuries East Ham was a quiet Essex agricultural village. There is archaeological evidence of a Roman settlement near the parish church of St Mary Magdalene and literary evidence that a village stood here in Saxon times. Recent discoveries of Bronze Age activity on East Ham's Thames-side marshes, including a wooden trackway, shed new light on prehistoric occupation of the area.

In the Middle Ages East Ham seems to have been a typical Essex village with no central settlement, but rather a scattering of isolated hamlets. These comprised South End, around the parish church; North End, along what is now High Street North; and Wall End, which lay towards the River Roding and Barking. Other settlements included Plashet and Green Street.

East Ham was to greatly increase in size. Little Ilford was a completely separate parish, one of the smallest in Essex, with its main settlements clustered around its own parish church of St Mary the Virgin and at Aldersbrook, where the City of London Cemetery now stands. Little Ilford did not join East Ham until 1886, when it became part of East Ham Sanitary District.

Much of the low-lying East Ham Levels in the south of the parish were included in Barking. The winding boundary stretching across the marshes probably reflected an earlier course of the Roding, which is also known as Barking Creek in its lower reaches. The Roding was not, in fact, established as the Barking-East Ham boundary until 1965.

Another anomaly was North Woolwich, which actually formed part of Kent rather than Essex until 1965. North Woolwich, comprising two detached riverside tracts, had probably been annexed to Kent by Hamon, Sheriff of Kent, in 1086, who may have added it to his estates south of the Thames to obtain ferry revenues.

In the earlier Middle Ages the great Forest of Essex (now called Epping Forest) stretched down as far as the Romford Road. This Roman road was the main east-west route until Barking Road was built in 1812. North-south routes were provided by White Post Lane (now High Street North) and its southern continuation, East Ham Manor Road (now High Street South), and by Gipsy Lane (now Green Street), which petered out in the southern marshes where it was known as Blind Lane. A small river, Ham Creek, was the boundary between East and West Ham, and here for a time in the seventeenth century there was a small naval base. Ham Creek is now entirely underground.

Unlike its neighbour West Ham, East Ham did not attract City merchants in the seventeenth and eighteenth centuries. Whereas in West Ham these wealthy men built themselves grand houses, in East Ham the families who lived in the big houses were never of more than local importance. Agriculture was the main occupation, although from the eighteenth century onwards the effect of London began to be felt as farms switched to potato-growing and market-gardening. Potato-growing attracted Irish immigrants, just one of the waves of newcomers which have periodically regenerated the area.

In the nineteenth century the East Ham Levels were transformed by industrial development. The Royal Group of Docks, begun in 1855, were partly in West Ham, with the Royal Albert (opened in 1880) and the King George V (opened in 1921) lying mainly on the East Ham side. The docks, together with Beckton Gasworks, begun in 1868, and Beckton Sewage Works, begun in 1890, brought thousands of newcomers to the area in search of work, and isolated estates such as Cyprus, Beckton and New Beckton grew up on the marshes.

In East Ham proper there was tremendous growth during the Victorian and Edwardian periods. Despite the riverside industries, East Ham was mainly a residential suburb, its neat redbrick terraces attracting bank clerks, well-to-do tradesmen and skilled artisans. Estates like Bonny Downs, Central Park, Manor Park and the Burges grew so quickly that in the 1890s East Ham was the fastest-growing town in Britain. There was always a friendly rivalry with East Ham's larger neighbour West Ham; fortunately East Ham escaped many of the social problems which occurred in West Ham as its bustling neighbourhoods developed in a more orderly fashion.

Orderly civic growth was definitely an abiding obsession of the early fathers of local government in East Ham. A local board was established in 1878 and East Ham became an urban district council in 1895, a municipal borough in 1904 and a county borough in 1915. Throughout these changes the chief concern was to avoid jerry-building and ensure adequate mains water and sewage connections. The guiding hand behind much of East Ham's growth at this time was John H. (later Lord) Bethell, who sat on all the local government bodies from the local board onwards. He pursued municipal development with energetic and visionary single-mindedness, including the acquisition of the site of the town hall and its construction. What now seems a handsome building fit for its purpose appeared to be an impossibly extravagant palace at its opening in 1903.

In the twentieth century East Ham has thrived as a pleasant suburb, proud of its shopping thoroughfares, civic institutions and busy social life. The Blitz led to large-scale evacuation and there was considerable bomb-damage, though not on the scale of West Ham. However, much needed to be rebuilt or repaired after the war. The postwar period was also characterized by fresh waves of immigration, this time from the Caribbean and south Asia, which have given the borough's streets and shops much more of a multicultural air. In 1965 East Ham was merged with its neighbour West Ham to become the London Borough of Newham.

Recently there have been large-scale changes in the south of East Ham, as industry has declined. The docks and the gasworks closed and the London Docklands Development Corporation was created amid political controversy to redevelop the area. New transport links were created, including the Docklands Light Railway and London City Airport, built on a derelict tongue of land between the Royal Albert and King George Docks. Much of Beckton, previously open land, was built over and new communities emerged with shops, schools and estates bringing new blood to the area.

SECTION ONE

EARLY HISTORY

Bronze Age spear from Thames-side marshes. There is some evidence of Stone Age settlement, but a remarkable collection of artefacts from the riverside marshes hints at an unusual level of activity during the Bronze Age. A recently-excavated wooden trackway led towards the river's edge, where fine spears (including the one shown here), swords and rapiers were deposited. This may have been a religious ritual in which symbols of power were dedicated to river gods.

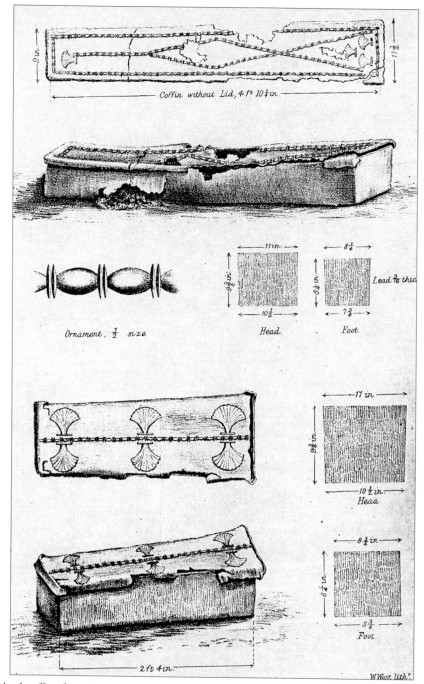

Roman lead coffins from East Ham. There was a small Roman settlement in East Ham near St Mary Magdalene Church. In 1863 workmen found evidence of Roman burials in what is now Roman Road. Three lead coffins were found and, after being displayed in the church porch, were sent to the British Museum from where they were unfortunately stolen in 1950.

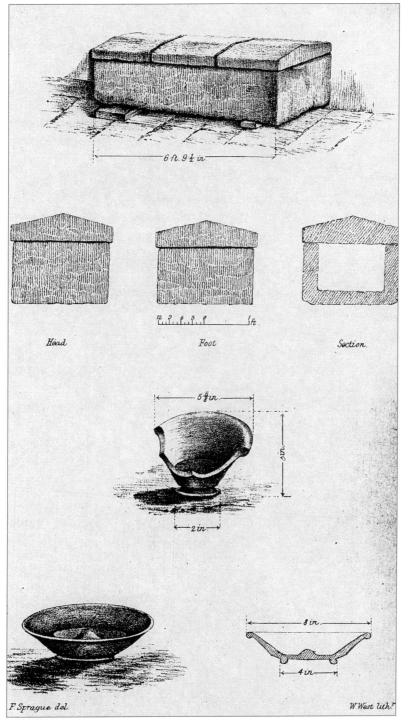

Roman stone coffin from East Ham. Also found was a stone coffin containing two skeletons, two wooden coffins, also 'occupied', some pottery and hipposandals – the Roman precursor of the horseshoe.

EÂDGÂR, 958.

✠ ANNO ab incarnatione domini nostri Ihesu Christi .DCCCC.LVIII. indictione .I. Ego Eadgar, allubescente gratia, rex et primicherius Mérciorum, aliquantulam ruris partem, quinis ab accolis aestimatam mansiunculis, in loco qui dicitur Hamme, Æðelstano comiti meo liberam, praeter arcem, pontem, expeditionemque, in perpetuum ius libenter admodum concedo; quatinus diebus uitae suae possideat, et post se cuicunque uoluerit haeredi derelinquat. Quod si quisque, quod non optamus, huiusce donationis cartulam adnichilare temptauerit, coram Christo se rationem redditurum agnoscat. Et his limitibus haec telluris pars circumgyrari uidetur. Ærest of Eádelmes díc on Stocfliót; of ðám flióte tó ilmére; andlang Wynsies mearce on ðone langan þorn; of ðám þornæ on wehincleáge; ðanon on Byrcmære; andlang mære on ðára hina mearcæ; andlang mearce tó Portan beorge; ðanon on Bædewyllan; andlang wylle ðæt innan hile; andlang ealdan hilæ æt ðæra hina mæde; ðanon innan fleót; andlang ðes fleótes on Træfesing múðan; andlang hile on Eádelmes díc. Et huius doni constipulatores exstiterunt quorum inferius nomina carraxari uidentur.

✠ Ego Oscitel episcopus consensi et subscripsi. ✠ Ego Dunstan episcopus consensi et subscripsi. ✠ Ego Cynesige episcopus consensi et subscripsi. ✠ Ego Aðulf episcopus consensi et subscripsi. ✠ Ego Ælfhere dux. ✠ Ego Æðelmund dux. ✠ Ego Æðelwold dux. ✠ Ego Birhtnoð dux. ✠ Ego Æðelsige minister. ✠ Ego Ælfsige minister. ✠ Ego Uffa minister. ✠ Ego Osferð minister. ✠ Ego Winsige minister. ✠ Ego Æðelwold minister. ✠ Ego Byrhtferð minister.

Rubric. Ðis is ðæra landbóc tó Hamme, ðæ Eádgár cing gebócade Æðelstáne bisceope on æce yrfe.

Saxon Charter of Hamme. By the late Saxon period there were several farming hamlets in the East Ham area, all administered as a single estate called Hamme, which included both East and West Ham. In AD 958 King Edgar granted this estate to his nobleman, Athelstan, and the Latin charter survives with the estate boundaries given in Anglo-Saxon.

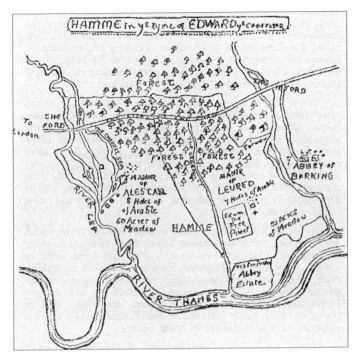

Hamme at the time of Edward the Confessor. This map is an imaginative reconstruction of the Hamme estate in about 1066 when it was divided between three landowners. Westminster Abbey owned a small riverside plot, which later became North Woolwich, technically part of Kent. Alestan held what later became West Ham, while Levred had East Ham. By 1086 these Saxon landowners had been replaced by Normans, Robert Gernon and Ranulph Peverel.

St Mary Magdalene, East Ham's parish church. The church occupies a strategic bluff overlooking the Thames and must lie very near if not over the small Roman settlement. A small church, probably timber, existed before the Norman Conquest as there is a reference in the Domesday Book to one Edwin, described as a 'free priest' who farmed a small plot of his own before 1066.

St Mary's Church, Little Ilford.
Little Ilford was eventually
absorbed by East Ham, but
began life as a separate parish
and, like East Ham, the church
originated with a pre-Norman
wooden building, traces of
which have been found during
excavations.

East Ham parish records. Minutes
of East Ham's vestry meetings – the
earliest form of parish government
– survive from 1736. Shown here
are the minutes of 12 August 1737.
Note the payments to various poor
women of the parish at the bottom
left.

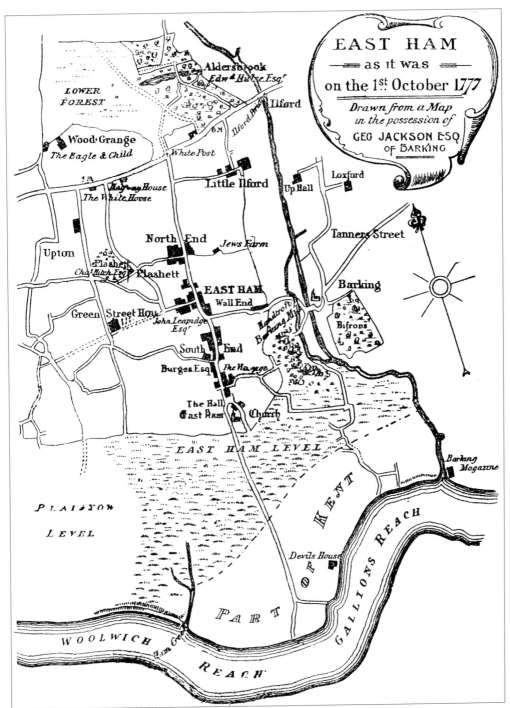

East Ham, 1777. By this time East Ham comprised a village nucleus along the present High Street with outlying hamlets (known as 'ends' in Essex) North End, South End and Wall End. Wall End acquired its name from the river wall that prevented the River Roding from flooding. Also marked is the district of Plashet, together with other scattered houses. The north end of the High Street was known as White Post Lane at this time.

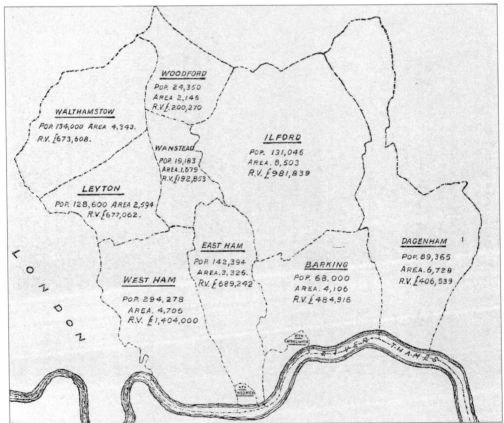

EAST HAM, 1860. P.O. DIRECTORY.

Private Residents—

Adams William, esq. Plashet hall.
Arnold Rev. John Muhleison, B.D.-P.H.D. curate. Villas.
Austin Mr. John, Oak Hall.
Boyle Revd. Edward Fitzmaurice, M.A.
Fry Mrs Henry, Grove cottage
Fry Mrs. William, Manor house
Garton Mr. John, Hawthorn cotttage
Gingell Jas esq. Wood house, North end.

Morley James esq, Greenstreet house.
Pelly Raymond esq J.P. Plashet house
Ramsden, Revd, Thomas Lagden, M.A. (Incumbent of Emmanuel church). North end.
Raven Mr. John
Taylor Henry esq.
Thomson George esq Rancliffe house
Venables Thomas esq Temple house

Commercial.

Abbot Jabez, market Gardener
Barnes, John, station master
Baskcombe Henry builder
Butler William Beer retailer
Carter, George, Dukes Head.
Carey, Stephen, manufacturer of animal charcoal. etc. Ilford Road
Circuit. Thos. farmer and market gardener.
Cloke Henry. sergeant of police
Cobb, William, market gardener
Collier. Thomas, baker
Cooper William shop keeper
Crowest Thomas, shoe maker
Dennison John Wm. architect and surveyor.
Dennisson, Thomas, wheelwright.
Forge Thomas, shop keeper
Harman, Robert, baker
Holloway Henry. cow keeper
Holloway William, farmer and market gardener.
Holmes William. Cock.
Hunt Thomas grocer
Keep John, beer retailer.
Lampard Thomas shop keeper

Lucy Joseph beer retailer
Lucy William, market gardener
Martin James, draper and post office
Meeks, Thomas, farm bailiff
Matthews Thomas and John, farmers
Mills, Thomas farmer and market gardener
Moss Henry, farmer
Moss James, farrior
Pearson Mrs. Sarah shop keeper
Perry William butcher
Pizzey Eliel. harness maker
Ramsden Joseph, farmer. Plashet
Reynolds John. beer retailer
Rust Mrs. Emily. farmer
Seabrook John Braley. White Horse
Smith. Henry. Dunn. beer retailer and bricklayer
Smith Robert. Rising Sun
Smith Thomas. beer retailer
Squire Mrs. Ann. wheelwright and carpenter
Stokes. William carpenter.
Styles, Mrs. Sarah, beer retailer
Vale John, market gardener.

East Ham, 1860. The Post Office Directory for 1860 shows East Ham to have been an unexceptional agricultural village with a typical mix of tradesmen, publicans and landowners.

East Ham and the surrounding area, 1931. East Ham grew with incredible rapidity between 1880 and 1914, transforming itself from a rural retreat to a major borough. It absorbed Little Ilford in 1886 and became one of the fastest-growing districts in England, swelling from 9,713 in 1881 to 69,758 in 1901, and from 69,758 in 1901 to 142, 394 in 1931.

CHURCHES

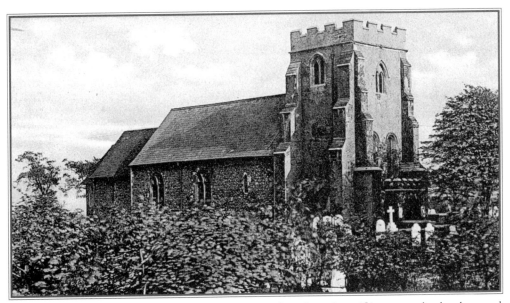

East Ham parish church. A fine Norman structure dating from the early twelfth century, the church escaped the clutches of Victorian restorers because the centre of population moved north. This left the church in a peripheral position and, instead of altering its interior, new churches were built in the town's new focus. The tower is thirteenth century.

East Ham parish church. This view shows the church from the south. The field from which the photograph was taken was eventually added to the churchyard, such was the demand for grave space. This enlarged the churchyard to 10½ acres, reputedly the largest in the country. The antiquarian William Stukeley (1687–1765) is buried here in an unmarked grave.

Double piscina, East Ham parish church. This unusual feature is located in the south wall of the apse.

Hermit's cell, East Ham parish church. A small chamber where a hermit once lived, has been cut into the north wall of the chancel. This is the exterior view; the hermit also had a small opening on the inside wall to allow him to see mass performed at the altar.

Font, East Ham parish church. The font is of white marble and was given by local landowner Sir Richard Heigham in 1639.

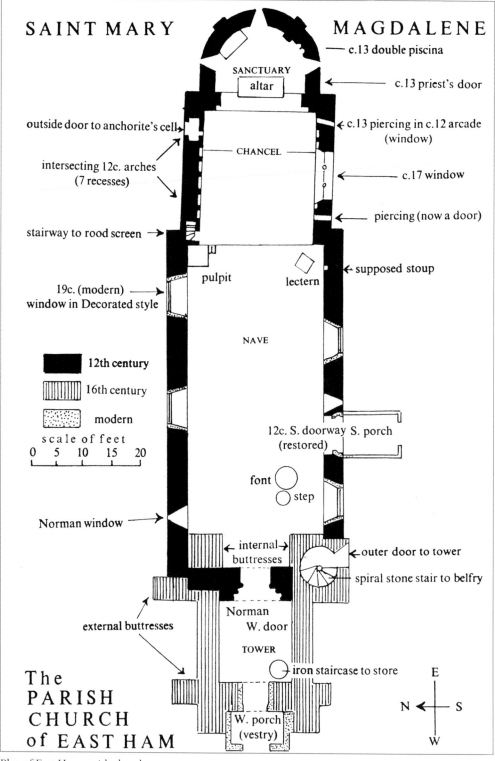

SAINT MARY   MAGDALENE

- c.13 double piscina
- c.13 priest's door
- c.13 piercing in c.12 arcade (window)
- c.17 window
- piercing (now a door)
- supposed stoup

SANCTUARY
altar

CHANCEL

outside door to anchorite's cell

intersecting 12c. arches (7 recesses)

stairway to rood screen

19c. (modern) window in Decorated style

NAVE

pulpit

lectern

■ 12th century

▥ 16th century

▦ modern

scale of feet
0   5   10   15   20

12c. S. doorway S. porch (restored)

font
step

Norman window

internal buttresses

outer door to tower

spiral stone stair to belfry

external buttresses

Norman W. door

TOWER

iron staircase to store

The PARISH CHURCH of EAST HAM

W. porch (vestry)

E
N ← + → S
W

Plan of East Ham parish church.

Little Ilford church. Like East Ham church, St Mary's, Little Ilford is mainly twelfth century, and has walls of plastered flint rubble. The south porch seen in this view is eighteenth century, as is the widened window adjacent.

Another view of Little Ilford church. The chancel was largely rebuilt in brick in the eighteenth century. The church is particularly associated with the Lethieullier family, who built a large vault and private chapel on the north side of the church in the eighteenth century which now serves as a vestry.

St John's Church, East Ham. As East Ham grew in the nineteenth century new churches were built in the centre of the district to serve the new estates and the original parish church of St Mary was left relatively isolated. This church, St John's, was erected in 1866 in High Street North, but was subsequently replaced by St Bartholomew's Church in 1902 and St John's served as a church hall. It was pulled down in 1925 and the site is now a car park.

St Stephen's Church, Green Street. Opened in 1887 to serve the Upton Park district, the church was a bastion of High Church Anglo-Catholicism. This view dates from about 1908. The church was destroyed in the Blitz.

St Barnabas's Church, Browning Road. Completed by 1906, St Barnabas's serves the Manor Park district.

St Michael's Church, Romford Road. Replacing an iron church built in 1898, this redbrick building was completed in 1912 and occupied a prominent site on the corner of Romford Road and Toronto Road. This postcard is postmarked 1916. The church was rebuilt on a smaller scale in the 1980s.

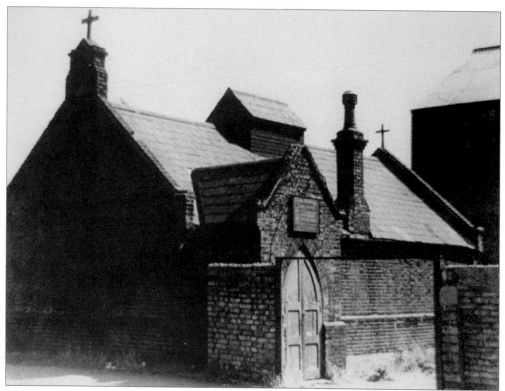

St Mark's, Cyprus. This tiny chapel was built in about 1890 in the isolated Cyprus estate (named to commemorate the capture of the island of Cyprus in 1878) on the Beckton marshes. The church was also close to the Beckton Gasworks and the Gas Light & Coke Company paid for an iron church hall in 1911. The church closed in 1952 and was demolished in the 1980s.

Methodist Central Hall, East Ham. This large Queen Anne-style building was the focus of Methodist activity in East Ham town centre. Methodism was a thriving denomination in the borough which long had a significant impact on local politics. Central Hall was opened in 1906 and seated over 2,000. A wide range of social activities took place at Central Hall; the Men's Brotherhood alone had 3,000 members in 1911, the date of this postcard. The building was demolished in 1969.

Plashet Grove Baptist Church. This large building, originally known as East Ham Tabernacle, was opened in 1901. Like Methodism, the Baptist cause was a significant one in East Ham life in the late nineteenth and early twentieth centuries, and during the Edwardian era this church regularly filled all 1,000 of its seats.

New Beckton Baptist Church. This iron church was built in 1888 in the Cyprus estate and was affectionately known locally as 'The Old Green Chapel'. Burnt down by arsonists in 1978, its altar cross was plucked from the flames and now stands in the new ecumenical church of St Mark, opened in 1987 in Tollgate Road, Beckton.

Plashet Park Congregational Church. Opened in 1887, this two-storey building was destroyed by bombing in 1941, but rebuilt and reopened in 1952.

DOCKS & INDUSTRY

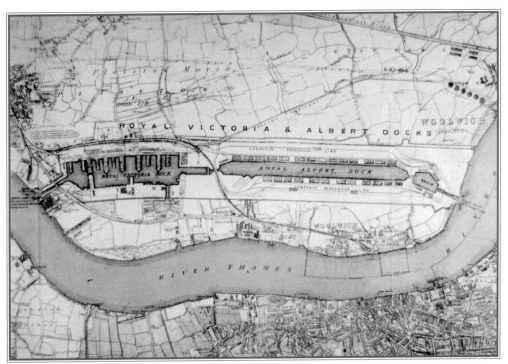

The Royal Docks. Unlike its industrial neighbour West Ham, East Ham was predominantly a residential borough. However, the presence of the Royal Docks in the south of the borough did act as a focus for some industrial activity and there was also some light industry in the north of the borough. The Royal Group of Docks were built piecemeal across empty marshland – the Royal Victoria in 1855, the Royal Albert in 1880 and the King George V (not shown on this plan) completed in 1921.

Aerial view of Royal Albert and King George V Docks. The vast capacity of the dockside transit sheds was staggering. The Royal Albert cold store alone could hold 4 million cubic feet of meat, mainly New Zealand mutton. The complex system of wharves and locks, cranes and railway lines, was highly mechanized, but still required a small army of men, many highly skilled, to keep it operating, and the docks was the largest single employer in East Ham.

Shipping lining the Royal Docks. The Royal Docks formed the largest artificial dock system in the world, with 93 hectares of enclosed water, nearly 18 km of quays and an internal railway system with 225 km of track. The Royal Albert Dock was 10 metres deep and could take ships up to 12,000 tonnes.

R. M. S. "Mauretania." Tonnage 32.000, Length 790 feet, Breadth 88 feet.

RMS *Mauretania*. The King George Dock could take even larger vessels. The biggest ever to visit the dock was the *Mauretania*, her 32,000 tonne bulk squeezing through the lock with just over 1 cm clearance on either side. The *Mauretania*'s visit in 1937 was treated as something of a local holiday and thousands turned out to watch the great liner edge into the dock.

A bustling scene at the Royal Albert Dock Basin. In their heyday shipping bound for the Royal Docks queued down the Thames as far as Southend-on-Sea, but containerization saw the focus of the Port of London's activity move to Tilbury Docks; the Royals began to decline and were closed in 1981. The water areas are now used for watersports, while London City Airport was opened in 1987 between the Royal Albert and King George V Docks.

Gray's timber merchant advertisement, *c.* 1920. The Royal Docks kept many small local businesses trading, including Gray's timber merchant of Katherine Road. The Royal Docks were not in fact as important as the Surrey Docks for timber imports, concentrating rather on frozen meat, tobacco and fruit.

Gaslight. A German inventor, Friedrich Albrecht Winzler, patented a method of extracting town gas from coal at the beginning of the nineteenth century. Coming to England to exploit his invention, he anglicized his name to Frederic Albert Winsor and founded the Gas Light & Coke Company in 1809. The first practical application of his invention was to provide street lighting, which caused astonishment in 1812 when it first appeared in Carlton House Terrace. In this cartoon Winsor, on the left, explains the principles to dubious onlookers. A candle-maker on the right mutters 'If this gas light is not put a stop to we must give up our business – we may as well shut up shop'.

Building Beckton Gasworks, 1869. By 1868 the Gas Light & Coke Company had grown so large it needed a new works to cope with demand. The spot selected was on remote marshland beside the Thames, partly in East Ham and partly in Barking. Work commenced in 1868 and the site was named Beckton in honour of the company's governor, Simon Adams Beck. This photograph shows the works under construction in 1869 and shortly after it was producing town gas for the capital.

Construction work at Beckton Gasworks. This photograph gives some idea of the Gothic splendour and the sheer scale of the original works.

Beckton Gasworks, 1881.

Aerial view of Beckton Gasworks. The plant was the largest gasworks in the world, employing thousands of local people, occupying an area the size of the City of London and serving 4½ million consumers in its heyday at the rate of 100,000,000 cubic feet of gas a day.

Beckton Gasworks, Riverside Piers. The Gas Light & Coke Company maintained its own riverside piers for unloading coal, which was brought to the piers by company ships at the rate of 1,700,000 tons a year. The coal was manually fed into furnaces for conversion into coke, with town gas as the by-product of this process.

Stokers in the retort house, Beckton Gasworks. The task of charging the retorts was hot, arduous and dangerous work. Coal was fed in on long-handled shovels and coke drawn out the same way.

General view of Beckton Gasworks. As well as the production of town gas, there was also a huge by-products works at Beckton. Tar, coke, fertilizers, ink, perfumes, medical products, dyes and even mothballs were all made at the by-products works, which were located where Beckton Retail Park now stands.

Beckton Alps. The gasworks were gradually run down in the 1970s as town gas was replaced by natural gas and most of its huge estate was sold off. Today housing covers much of the western half of the site. Imaginative use was made of the slag heap – it was grassed over and turned into an artificial ski slope and renamed 'Beckton Alps'!

When Your Ship Comes Home

You have dreams of a life of ease; a home where comfort dwells; security for you and yours from the cares of the world.

But why wait for the ship? Till it comes, enjoy the comforts that require no royal riches—the comforts that every home can have.

Radiant warmth in every room; beautiful and adequate lighting, free from glare; gloriously hot baths at will, and an ample supply of hot water for all other needs; punctual and perfectly cooked meals.

These are the comforts that Gas brings to the home—by means of Gas Fires, Gas Cooker, Gas Water-Heaters, Gas Lighting. All will help to make your home plane sailing, running as smoothly as the ship of your dreams.

Let us advise and assist you to make your home a home where comfort dwells.

THE GAS LIGHT & COKE COMPANY
HORSEFERRY ROAD, WESTMINSTER, S.W.1

Gas Light & Coke Company advertisement, 1925.

Burgoyne's advertisement, 1939. The manufacture of medical products was mainly associated with West Ham rather than East Ham, but Burgoyne's was an interesting exception. The company's distinctive redbrick works in High Street South remains a significant local landmark, though it has long since closed

Beckton Sewage Works. Pollution and disease were endemic in London until the late nineteenth century, chiefly as a result of poor sewage disposal. Civil engineer Joseph Bazalgette devised a brilliantly simple plan by which all London's sewage would be drawn out of the capital by feeder pipes into two great sewers, one north and one south of the river. The Northern Outfall Sewer was built in 1864 and crossed East Ham to pour its filth into the Thames at Creekmouth. Sewage treatment was not provided until 1889, but has been continuously improved since then until today Beckton Sewage Works is the largest in the country and one of the largest in the world.

Gallions Pumping Station, 1970s. Redevelopment of Docklands over the last twenty-five years has necessitated major improvements to the drainage system because much of Beckton lies below sea level. A series of deep storm sewers was constructed in the 1970s with huge surface-level pumping stations to ensure that flooding cannot occur.

Robertson & Woodcock horse and carriage, c. 1910. Robertson & Woodcock founded their confectionery business in Shaftesbury Road in 1907, adopting the brand name 'Trebor' (the first letters of Robertson reversed). At first their distribution network was by horse and cart. Soon after, however, the company equipped themselves with a fleet of motor trucks.

Robertson & Woodcock motor lorry, *c.* 1915.

Trebor Works. As the company expanded a new art deco-style works was built in 1937. The company moved their operations out of the borough in the 1980s and the works now houses small businesses and light industry units.

HOUSES

Boleyn Castle, 1904. This extraordinary building, part of Green Street House, was the subject of much local legend. By tradition Anne Boleyn lived here and Henry VIII courted her there in secret trysts. The house and 'castle' were probably built in the early sixteenth century by Richard Breame, one of Henry VIII's courtiers. Breame also had a house in Greenwich rented by Henry for the use of Lord Rochford, Anne Boleyn's brother, and this is probably the origin of the legend. The building was demolished in 1955.

Another view of Boleyn Castle, 1932. Despite the lack of documentary evidence about the Anne Boleyn connection, local streets in Upton Park were named after contemporaries of Henry VIII. The upper castellated part of the tower was rebuilt in about 1800.

Boleyn Castle. This view shows the reformatory built after Cardinal Manning acquired the site for the Roman Catholic Church in 1869.

Green Street House. The detached 'castle' can be seen on the left. The house itself comprised a great hall with cross-wings at either end.

Green Street House. The house was used by the Catholic Church as a maternity home and later became a social club. After the war the house became very run down and was demolished in 1955.

Little Ilford Manor House. The octagonal roof lantern was a common feature of larger local houses and enabled residents to watch shipping on the Thames. The house, which had been demolished by 1901, seems to have been of eighteenth-century origin, though it may have had a core dating back to the sixteenth or seventeenth century. It stood at what is now the junction of Church Road and Dersingham Avenue.

Manor House, Manor Park, *c.* 1900. Not to be confused with Little Ilford Manor House, this building stands in Gladding Road and gave its name to Manor Park. Built some time between 1810 and 1827 by West Ham's lord of the manor, it was sold to the Catholic Church in 1868, who used it as a school. In 1925 it was sold to the Co-op and the building was used as offices for many years until 1989, when it was restored and converted into flats.

Oak Hall. This early eighteenth-century house once stood at the corner of East Ham High Street and Wakefield Street. Demolished in about 1935, the property is remembered by older local residents as 'Dr Beaumont's' as it functioned as a doctor's surgery after the First World War.

The Limes. This large house stood between White Post Lane (now High Street North), Gladstone Avenue and Jews Farm Lane (now East Avenue) and, like Oak Hall, dated from the eighteenth century. Towards the end of the nineteenth century it was the residence of Joseph East, first Chairman of East Ham Urban District Council (in whose honour Jews Farm Lane was renamed). For a short time it served as a temporary library for northern East Ham, while Plashet Library was under construction.

Wood House. Commemorated in the name Woodhouse Grove, Wood House was an eighteenth century building which stood in Plashet. It was unusual in that it was weatherboarded and may have been timber built throughout. The grounds of Wood House were purchased in 1889 and opened as Plashet Park in 1891, East Ham's earliest municipal park, and the house was subsequently demolished.

Staircase of Rancliffe House. Yet another large early eighteenth-century house in East Ham. Quite a number of these similarly-styled gentlemen's residences were built at that time and acted as country retreats for city merchants. This view shows the staircase in 1908. The house was demolished after the grounds were opened as Central Park in 1898.

Round House. Demolished in 1894, this house stood in Plashet Grove. There are a number of round houses in south Essex, usually associated with Dutch settlement, but this house is in fact octagonal and was built to house four separate families.

Plashet House. This house was mentioned as early as 1619 and passed through the hands of the Bendish and Hitch families, both prominent in local affairs. It passed to the Fry family, who owned it from 1784 to 1829, when they moved to West Ham. This sketch was made by Elizabeth Fry's daughter, Katharine. The estate was sold for development in 1883 and the house was demolished three years later.

Plashet Cottage. Near Plashet House stood Plashet Cottage which became the home of Katharine Fry. A keen local historian, she wrote a history of East and West Ham and her entertaining and delightfully illustrated journal was published this century as *Katharine Fry's Book*. Her cottage became well known as the venue for 'essay meetings', comprising readings and poetry.

Potato Hall. This late eighteenth-century house stood on the corner of what is now Romford Road and Katherine Road and possessed a lookout tower like several other large houses in the area.

THE MUNICIPAL JOURNAL

ESTABLISHED AS "LONDON" ELEVENTH YEAR OF ISSUE

No. 530.—Vol. XII.   MARCH 27, 1903.

ENTERPRISE AT EAST HAM.

A £120,000 Housing Scheme the Latest Undertaking.—The Class of Persons Catered for.—A Visit to the Dwellings.

AN admirable progressive spirit animates East Ham in regard to municipal matters. Only a few weeks ago we recorded the opening of an extremely handsome Town Hall and a commodious suite of new offices for housing the

housing scheme, Mr. Campbell thinks that there need not arise those fears of interference with private enterprise which have been so frequently exploited lately by opponents of so-called municipal trading.

The class of persons generally reached by private enterprise are those in receipt of good wages, and able to pay rents of (in London suburbs) from 7s. per week upwards. This standard, of course, varies with the district, its rates of wages, costs of living, &c., but Mr. Campbell thinks it may be assumed, as a rule, that any inclusive rent exceeding one shilling a day becomes burdensome to the class of tenant sought to be catered for by a local authority in providing dwellings for the labouring classes. If, then, the rate of one shilling a day were adopted as the maximum rent which should be charged, a necessary preliminary to the size and character of a house would thus be determined. This course has been followed in connection with the East Ham scheme, and Mr. Campbell has found that for each 100ft. of available floor space in rooms (excluding lobbies, passages, and closets) a rental of from 1s. 4d. to 1s. 7d. per week is required, according to the economy and plan adopted.

But to come to the East Ham scheme proper. The urgency of providing accommodation for the labouring classes was first brought under notice by the sanitary inspector, who in several of his reports

THE SAVAGE GARDENS DWELLINGS.

Municipal housing, Savage Gardens. East Ham was in the forefront of council house provision and constructed 132 well-built dwellings in Beckton's Savage Gardens and a further 80 in Brooks' Avenue (which survive). The opening ceremony in 1903 attracted considerable interest, not least from *The Municipal Journal*.

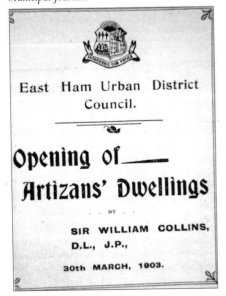

East Ham Urban District Council.

Opening of Artizans' Dwellings

BY

SIR WILLIAM COLLINS, D.L., J.P.,

30th MARCH, 1903.

Opening programme for the Savage Gardens municipal housing development.

INNS

The Black Lion. A down-to-earth early nineteenth-century pub which formerly stood in High Street North, opposite the Harrow inn *(see p. 59).*

The Boleyn Tavern. This florid Edwardian pub stands on the corner of Barking Road and Green Street.

The Coach and Horses. It is still standing in Romford Road and still serving the needs of thirsty local residents just as it has done since it was a coaching inn.

The Connaught Tavern and cast-iron urinal. The Connaught, strictly speaking in West Ham, was a well-known dockers' watering hole built in 1881 by Vigers and Wagstaffe, who were responsible for several important dock buildings. The pub was closed at the end of the 1980s and the adjacent Board of Trade building, in similar style, was demolished. The cast-iron urinal in the foreground is a listed building in its own right, one of the last of its type in the country.

The Denmark Arms. This Edwardian building stands at the crossroads of High Street North and Barking Road and thus at the heart of East Ham life. This is the second pub on the site; the earlier Denmark, built in the 1870s, was a plainer affair.

An unusual shot of the saloon bar of the Denmark Arms in 1909. A spittoon stands in front of the ornate bar.

The Duke of Edinburgh. This pub stands on the corner of Green Street and Plashet Grove.

The Ferndale. Built in the 1880s to serve the Cyprus estate, the pub is the only surviving building from the original Cyprus estate, which was demolished and rebuilt in the 1980s.

The Gallions Hotel. Mentioned in Kipling's yarn *The Light That Failed*, Gallions was built between 1881 and 1883 by Vigers and Wagstaffe to serve a luxury liner trade that never in fact developed from the Royal Docks. The Port of London Authority Railway had its terminus here.

The Green Man, a mid-nineteenth-century inn straddling the junction of Plashet Grove and Katherine Road.

The Three Rabbits. Named after an extensive warren which once stood nearby on (Epping) forest land, an inn of this name dates back at least as far as the eighteenth century. At that time a huge annual cattle fair used to be held on Wanstead Flats and the pub became the focus for much of the dealing.

The Gallions Hotel. After its closure in 1972, Gallions rapidly became derelict, its roof tiles smashed by vandals and its heroic plaster frieze crumbling. However, it has recently been restored to something like its original splendour, although a long-term use has yet to be found for it.

The Harrow. This building probably dates back to the sixteenth century and gave its name to Harrow Road (which now forms part of Ron Leighton Way). In the nineteenth century the inn was turned into a private house and later demolished. A small green in front of the inn was once the site of East Ham's stocks.

The White Horse. This thatched inn dated from the eighteenth century and stood on the corner of
Rancliffe Road, now occupied by the gates into Central Park. The pub was rebuilt across the road on the
east side of High Street South in 1905 and rebuilt again in 1965.

PEOPLE

Robert Banks-Martin. Alderman Banks-Martin JP was East Ham's longest-serving mayor, having carried that office throughout the difficult years of the First World War. During this time his well-known 'stiff upper lip' carried the council through dark hours when many hundreds of young East Ham men were being slaughtered in Flanders fields.

Sir Joseph Bazalgette, the civil engineer who conceived the idea of the Northern and Southern Outfall Sewers; the Northern Outfall Sewer bisects East Ham as it carries sewage from London out to Beckton and thence into the Thames. Bazalgette's best known work is, however, the Thames Embankment, where a monument to his memory still stands.

Simon Adams Beck, governor of the Gas Light & Coke Company 1860–76. As governor, Beck drove in the first pile of the new river wall on 19 November 1868 and the following day it was 'Resolved that the Company's property at Galleon's Reach near Barking be henceforth called Beckton'. Beckton Gasworks soon grew to become the largest in the world.

Dr W. Benton, the much-respected Medical Officer of Health for East Ham, 1908–33. He later served as a Justice of the Peace.

John Henry Bethell, later Lord Bethell (1861–1945). Bethell was the founding father of modern East Ham, energetically promoting the town and its development. He served as mayor in 1904–5 and again in 1905–6, having already served as Urban District Council Chairman in 1897–8. He received a knighthood and the Freedom of the Borough in 1906 and a baronetcy in 1911, followed by a peerage in 1922, having served as MP for Romford 1906–18 and MP for East Ham North 1918–22.

Colonel Ynyr Henry Burges. The Burges family were East Ham's biggest landowners and the development of their estates from about 1890 to 1914 transformed the village into a town. The biggest block of land lay to the east of the High Street; this development is still known as the Burges estate. In recognition of his role in the town's growth, Colonel Ynyr Burges was made charter mayor of East Ham in 1904, the year the town became a municipal borough.

Jack Cornwell VC (1900–16). Cornwell, of Alverstone Road, Little Ilford, joined the Navy in 1915 with the rank of 'Boy, 1st Class'. On board the HMS *Chester* during the Battle of Jutland he was hit and fatally wounded while on duty beside a gun. However, he remained at his post and died shortly afterwards. For his steadfastness he was awarded the VC and for many years every classroom in the country was supposed to have a picture of the boy hero as an example and inspiration.

David Farrar (1908–95). Born in Forest Gate, Farrar was a popular screen idol of the 1940s. His best known starring roles were in *Meet Sexton Blake* (1944), *Black Narcissus* (1946) and *The Small Back Room* (1948).

EXPECTING A JOYFVL RESVRRECTION
HERE RESTETH Y·BODY OF ELIZABETH Y ELDEST
DAVGT OF IAMES HARVEY OF DAGENHAM IN THE
COVNTY OF ESSEX ESQ· AND LATELY Y VERTVOVS
LOVING & MOST BELOVED·WIFE OF RICHᴰ HEIGHAM
OF EASTHAM IN YE SAID COVNTY OF ESSEX,ESQVIEP
BY WHOM SHE HAD ISSVE,ONE SONNE AND TWO
DAVGHTᴿ Y IS TO SAY,IAMES,MARIE,& ELIZABETH,AND
DEPARTED THIS LIFE RIGHT GODLY & CHRISTIANLY Y
Iᴰ DAY OF IVLY THE YEARE AFTER Y INCARNATION
OF OVR SAVIOR CHRIST 1622

Elizabeth Heigham (*d.* 1622). This memorial brass in East Ham church commemorates the wife of Sir Richard Heigham; the Heighams were a prominent local family.

Dame Vera Lynn (1917–). Well known as the 'Forces Sweetheart' during the Second World War, this singer was born in Thackeray Road and first took to the stage as a child at local talent contests in East Ham.

Edgar Kinghorne Myles (1894–1977), another East Ham war hero. Born in Milton Avenue, he served at Gallipoli and later went to Mesopotamia where, at the Battle of Sanna-i-Yat in 1916, he rescued wounded men in no man's land while under heavy Turkish fire for which he won the VC. His outstanding bravery was repeated in 1917 at the Battle of Kut and he won the DSO.

HERE LYETH THE BODY OF HESTER NEVE DE
VARTVOVS LOVEINGE AND OBEDYENT WIFE
OF FRANCIS NEVE GTEZEN AND MARCHANT
TAYLOR OF LONDON SHEE DEPARTED THIS
LIFE THE EYGHT DAYE OF JVLY AN DNI 1610
OM OR ABOWGT THE 58 YEARE OF HER AGE

Hester Neve (1552–1610). This illustration is taken from her monumental brass which lies in the chancel of East Ham church.

Alfred Stokes, Mayor of East Ham, 1922–3, and author of the most detailed local history of East Ham, the third edition published in 1933 under the title *East Ham: From Village to County Borough*.

The Reid family. Left to right: Thomas Reid snr, Thomas Reid jnr, William Reid and John Reid. Originally from Scotland, the Reids moved south to East Ham and after some time at the Thames Iron Works they began building houses. Many Reid houses survive in Central Park Road and area. John Reid was for a time a missionary in what is now Botswana, where he was attacked in the bush by a leopard which tore off his eyelid.

Will Thorne (1857–1946). After walking to East Ham from Birmingham to find work, the young Will Thorne took up employment at Beckton Gasworks. There, in a campaign to improve conditions, he founded the Gas Workers' Union and in 1891 he became a West Ham councillor. Later he was MP for West Ham South, 1906–18 and Plaistow 1918–45. The Gas Workers' Union went on to become the GMB, now one of Britain's largest unions.

Dick Turpin (1705–39). Born in Hempstead, Essex, the most notorious of highwaymen eventually hanged at York for his misdeeds. According to popular legend he committed some of his earliest cattle-rustling and horse-stealing exploits on the East Ham Levels (now Beckton) and later married an East Ham girl named Hester Palmer who lived in Market Street. His wife was actually named Elizabeth Millington.

Frederic Winsor. Born in Bavaria as Friedrich Albrecht Winzler, his founding of the Gas Light & Coke Company was ultimately to have a profound effect on East Ham in general and Beckton in particular.

Cartoon of Frederic Winsor. In this cartoon Winsor is being lampooned for his initial failure to raise money to exploit his new invention of town gas. One disgruntled onlooker says 'Don't believe what he says, it's all smoke', while another one moans, 'D . . n your gas pipes I say! You are so frequently breaking up the pavement that there is no such thing as walking the streets upon clean legs without a pair of stilts!'

PUBLIC SERVICES & UTILITIES

East Ham Town Hall, c. 1905. A local government board was first set up in East Ham in 1878, which absorbed the previously separate parish of Little Ilford in 1886. In 1895 East Ham became an urban district council and this coincided with the town's rapid growth. Dominating local politics was John (later Lord) Bethell who strove ceaselessly to advance the town's development.

East Ham Town Hall, *c.* 1928. By 1904 the town became a municipal borough and this was followed by county borough status in 1915.

East Ham Town Hall, *c.* 1945. The town hall site, at the very heart of East Ham, was purchased for £80,000 at the turn of the century and the building opened in 1903. A striking and stately building, it dominates yet is complemented by the surrounding suite of buildings, which include the fire station, library, police station and technical college, some of which have been rebuilt or converted to other uses since their construction.

East Ham's coat of arms. This emblem was used from 1904, originally without heraldic authority. The three torches represent Beckton Gasworks, the ship represents the docks, while the crozier represents the church, and in particular, William de Monfichet's grant of the manor of East Ham to Stratford Langthorne Abbey.

East Ham Fire Brigade. East Ham's first fire brigade was composed of volunteers, but in 1897 the Urban District Council established the full-time crew seen here at the fire station behind the original council offices in Wakefield Street. The brigade was equipped with this splendid horse-drawn steam fire engine.

East Ham Fire Station. A new fire
station was built adjacent to the town
hall in 1914 and the internal
combustion engine replaced
horsepower. This building is now in
use as council offices.

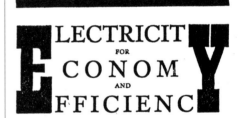

East Ham Electricity Department advertisement.
Like many other municipal authorities, East Ham
had its own electricity undertaking, set up in 1901
and supplying most domestic consumers in the
borough by 1936. This was something of an uphill
struggle given the close proximity of Beckton
Gasworks and hence local loyalty to gas supply. The
electricity undertaking was nationalized in 1947.

East Ham Library. East Ham's first library opened in 1896 in North Woolwich, followed by Plashet Library in 1898 and Manor Park in 1905. In 1908 East Ham Central Library was finally completed, funded by philanthropist Andrew Carnegie and bearing the coat of arms of his home town, Dunfermline, on its portico. This photograph from 1908 was taken before the town hall extension was built in 1910.

East Ham Public Baths

These modern Baths, conveniently situated next to the Town Hall in the centre of the Borough offer every facility for recreation, athletic exercise and health-giving treatment.

The accommodation provided is:—

Swimming Bath

Pond, 120 ft. × 40 ft., with diving pool 8 ft. 4 in. deep in centre, designed to the requirements of the Amateur Diving Association.

Slipper Baths

Eighteen in number.

Medicated Vapour Baths

Equipped with latest fittings and furnishings, and comprising: Three Steam Rooms, Plunge Bath, Needle Bath, Showers, Spinal Douche Shampooing Room and spacious Cooling Room adequately furnished for comfort of bathers. Refreshments can be obtained at popular prices.

FOR THE HOURS OF OPENING AND ADMISSION CHARGES SEE POSTERS

East Ham Public Baths advertisement. The swimming baths were slotted into a narrow site behind the library and town hall in 1912, replacing an open-air baths in Central Park. East Ham Baths were closed by Newham Council in the 1980s.

The old workhouse. This pair of cottages in Wall End — that 'end' nearest Barking — was leased by the parish council in 1804 and ten years later was accommodating twenty-five paupers. In 1827 a new workhouse was built in Wakefield Street, then in 1836 East Ham became part of the West Ham Poor Law Union, using that union's facilities, which lay outside the parish.

City of London Cemetery. Occupying the former Aldersbrook estate in Little Ilford, this huge necropolis was opened in 1857. The design, by William Haywood, incorporated curvilinear roads leading to three denominational chapels.

Passmore Edwards Hospital, 1906. The hospital, in Shrewsbury Road, was opened in 1902 after philanthropist Passmore Edwards had donated £5,000.

St John's Ambulance Brigade, East Ham Division, 1905. Founded in 1895, the ladies of the St John's Ambulance Brigade undertook valuable nursing services in the borough.

East Ham Memorial Hospital during Queen Mary's formal tour of inspection on the opening day, 24 July 1929. This much larger hospital was constructed adjacent to Passmore Edwards Hospital.

SCHOOLS

Shaftesbury Road School. East Ham established a school board in 1873. One of the earliest elementary schools to be built was Shaftesbury Road School, opened in 1894 and still in use, although it suffered a disastrous fire in 1904 and had to be largely rebuilt.

East Ham Technical College. This sumptuously ornate redbrick and terracotta building opened in 1905 and served as the venue for both evening classes and a secondary school. In 1962 the college moved to a site in High Street South opposite the town hall, where, now known as Newham Community College, it occupies a strikingly modernist building.

Doorway of East Ham Technical College. This close-up shows the magnificent detail of the terracotta moulding and wrought ironwork.

St Edward's Roman Catholic Reformatory School. Opened in 1870 close to Boleyn Castle and built in deliberate imitation of the 'castle', the school was part of the large-scale Catholic mission organized by Cardinal Manning after 1869. Closed in 1906, the school later became an electrical works, Browning's factory.

Waldstein Academy of Music. This advertisement from 1920 promotes one of a plethora of similar small private institutions flourishing in the area.

SECTION NINE

SHOPS & SHOPPING

*The Co-op Store, c. 1954. Built on the site of St John's
Church, East Ham Co-op opened on 25 April 1928 and
was a prominent town centre landmark. Closed in 1983,
this fine art deco building was eventually demolished to
make way for a car park.*

R. C. FISH

PAWNBROKER, JEWELLER AND GENERAL SALESMAN.

Money Lent at
Lowest Interest

ON

Jewellery, Plate. Furniture, Pianos, Bicycles, and every description of Property.

THE NOTED
'BARGAIN SHOP'

GRAND VALUE IN NEW & SECOND-HAND JEWELLERY, Diamond Rings, Bracelets, Watches, Wedding Rings & Keepers, Cutlery and Plate.

Large Stock of New and Second-hand Furniture, Carpets, Lino and Rugs

CLOTHING, FURS, BOOTS, TABLE LINEN, BLANKETS, SHEETS, Etc.

Note Address: – **R. C. FISH,**

25 & 27, High Street,
And at 101/103, Burdett Rd. E. and 49/51, Hornsey Rd. N. **N. East Ham**

An advertisement for Fish's jeweller's. One of East Ham's oldest established jewellers in the town centre, Fish's still thrives in the High Street. This advertisement dates from about 1920.

Burton's. The Burton chain of gentlemen's outfitters originated in 1900 when Maurice Burton emigrated to Britain from Lithuania. He soon established a chain of shops with distinctive frontages, like this one in East Ham High Street.

An advertisement for Lank's confectioner's, *c.* 1920. A
well-known and much-loved local store, alas no longer
with us.

Larkin's Confectioner's, 1930. The Larkin family were well known in both East and West Ham and had
shops in both boroughs, including this High Street sweet shop.

Bailey Brothers advertisement. A 1955 advertisement for Bailey's drapery store.

The Manor Park Dairy. Many such small dairies once existed in East Ham, some with yards behind where live cattle were kept. The Manor Park Dairy stood at 32 Station Road, close to Manor Park station. A typical delivery cart with shiny churns and a smartly turned out delivery 'boy' stands on the left, while in the doorway the proprietor, George Gilbert, looks on proudly.

An advertisement for Tricker's Merchant Tailor's, *c.* 1920. Note the emphasis on naval uniforms, important in a dockside borough like East Ham.

Buttrey's Wool Shop advertisement, 1939. Buttrey's Wool Shop is still thriving in East Ham and celebrates its centenary in 1997.

Reader's Dairy, also known as Durham Cross Dairy, situated at 570 Romford Road between High Street
North and Salisbury Road, and clearly a business on a much larger scale than the Manor Park Dairy (see
p. 86). Note the common boast 'Families waited on three times daily', a necessity to ensure freshness in
the days before domestic refrigeration.

An advertisement for Seff's Hairdresser's, 1939;
note the prices.

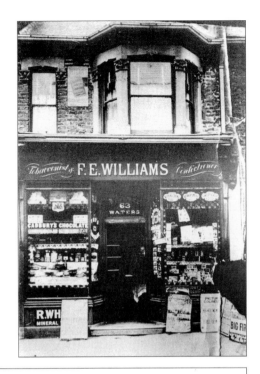

Williams' Tobacconist. This shop stood in Plashet Grove. The shop owner was Florence E. Williams, who ran it from 1922 until her death in 1928. Most East Ham streets had a corner store like this between the wars.

ESTABLISHED 1899.

A. D. DEATH

Imperial Cigar Stores

313 HIGH STREET, NORTH

MANOR PARK. - - - - LONDON, E.12

CIGARS OF ALL — BRANDS —

CIGARETTES BY WEIGHT.

A good Stock of Pipes, Pouches, Sticks, &c.

TRY MY
" HONEYSWEET MIXTURE "
10d. oz. AND YOU WILL LIKE IT. 10d. oz.

Advertisement for Death's Tobacconist. Dating from 1924, the irony of the shopowner's name was probably lost on readers of this advertisement.

Staff of Arthy's Bakery, *c.* 1900. Standing proudly in their yard at 427 High Street, these aproned bakers could hardly have predicted that the family firm of Arthy would still be going strong nearly a century later.

THE "BEEHIVE" FISH STORES

Late " OLD COMRADES " FISH SHOP
Under entirely NEW MANAGEMENT

Best Quality Fish, all varieties at Lowest Prices.

Try our Home Cured Haddocks and Bloaters—the work of experts.

TEST OUR FRIED FISH

A qualified chef has been specially engaged for this side of our business: therefore an appetising and nutritious lunch or supper is assured.

Try our special POTATO FRITTERS. A treat for young and old.
Frying daily   -   -   12—2 & 7—11.
Our Motto—To Please and Satisfy—A trial will convince you

357, KATHERINE ROAD

An advertisement for the Beehive Fish Stores. Fish and chips seem to have been treated as something of a gourmet meal by this fish shop at least, if this 1924 advertisement is to be believed.

Burnett's Bakery cart, *c.* 1912. Unlike Arthy's, Burnett's Bakery has disappeared. It was located near the Princess Alice public house at 327 Romford Road. The ornately-painted handcart is typical of the period in which the photograph was taken. The delivery boy is Edwin Spraggs, who was born in 1895 and died in 1925 as a result of tuberculosis contracted in the First World War.

Quebec Radio Shop advertisement, 1939. At this time every home aspired to have its own wireless set, particularly to hear the latest news as war clouds gathered over Europe.

Davies' Removals advertisement, 1955. This is a recent reminder of the tenacity of place names. Wall End had once marked the outlying hamlet or 'end' of East Ham which stood close to Barking Creek. By 1955 this area was of course entirely built up, but the name persists to this day to define the area round the Duke's Head pub.

Beckton District Centre. The modern face of shopping is the out-of-town superstore and mall and East Ham has its own versions of these at the Beckton District Centre and the Savacentre superstore in East Beckton. Beckton District Centre opened in September 1983 and includes a supermarket (Asda) and a pub (the Tollgate Tavern). As the retail boom developed in the 1980s the light industrial units of the nearby London Industrial Park were transformed into Beckton Retail Park, while the Savacentre opened in October 1993.

SOCIAL LIFE

Plashet Park. The first municipal park in East Ham, Plashet Park was opened to the public in 1891 on land which had formerly been part of the Wood House estate (see p. 46). In this scene a young family pose for the camera in about 1900. The houses of Plashet Grove can be seen in the background.

Plashet Park, photographed from a similar viewpoint as the previous picture, but in the 1960s.

Royal Victoria Gardens, North Woolwich. This riverside park was originally laid out as a private pleasure gardens in 1853 by the entrepreneur William Holland, but by the time this view was taken in about 1905 the park had been purchased by East Ham Council.

Royal Victoria Gardens, North Woolwich. Its latter years as a pleasure garden were clouded by what local historian Alfred Stokes described as an 'undesirable reputation'. Steamers from Tower Pier brought boatloads of intoxicated Cockneys in search of dubious pleasures and local reaction was strong. £20,000 was raised by public subscription and the park was brought into public ownership in 1890.

Beckton Park, *c.* 1903, shortly after the park opened. The houses of Savage Gardens can be seen on the left. Swans sail serenely on the lake in front of the bandstand.

Beckton Park. The park was extensively refurbished in the early 1980s when the area was developed for housing by London Docklands Development Corporation. After some years of decline new trees and shrubs were planted and sports facilities were upgraded.

Stroud Pavilion, Beckton Park. The Stroud Pavilion houses changing rooms, there is a bowling green adjacent. The park formed part of a much larger open space, Beckton District Park, which virtually encircles new housing estates built in the 1980s.

Programme from East Ham Palace. The East Ham Palace was the last surviving theatre in East Ham. Built in about 1906 on the corner of Burges Road and High Street North, it endured the Blitz and lasted until 1956, by which time it had acquired a rather sleazy reputation. The variety programme on offer on 21 April 1947 included 'Stephane Grapelly' (sic), described as the 'World's Greatest Swing Violinist' and Max Miller, the immensely popular risqué comedian.

Co-op outing. With improved roads, the era of the charabanc dawned and on summer weekends the roads to Southend, Clacton and Margate bustled with motor coaches. A huge array of social groups, ranging from temperance organizations to drinking clubs, hired charabancs for day trips out of East Ham. Here we see a London Co-operative Society outing in about 1920, leaving from the Co-op's Flanders Road office.

Mansfield House
Players

at

East Ham Town Hall.

SEASON   -   -   1925-6.

"FANNY'S FIRST PLAY"
1st & 2nd Oct.   G. B. Shaw.

"THE LIKES OF HER"
12th & 14th Nov.   McEvoy.

"CROMWELL"
2nd & 7th Jan.   M. Drinkwater.

"The GREAT ADVENTURE"
11th & 13th Feb.   Arnold Bennett.

"ST. JOAN" or
      "MAJOR BARBARA"
11th & 13th March.   G. B. Shaw.

Inc. Tax
Season Tickets for the 5 plays - 5,9
  ,,   ,, num. & reserved 10/-
Tickets for each Performance at
Popular Prices.

Doors open 7 p.m.   Commence 7.30

Mansfield House Players advertisement, *c.* 1925. Social life thrived in East Ham between the wars, with amateur dramatics just one aspect of a very broad tapestry.

Wanstead Fair, 1907. Originating as a busy cattle market, Wanstead Fair gradually developed into a purely pleasure fair, traditionally held at Easter. Although it died out during the First World War, the fair has been revived in recent years.

STREETS & VIEWS

High Street North, c. 1905. A general view looking north with the Ruskin Arms pub on the right.

High Street North, *c.* 1905. Another view with shop fronts hidden behind their white blinds. This end of the High Street was formerly known as White Post Lane because of a marker post which once stood at the junction with Romford Road.

High Street North. At the junction with Tennyson Avenue (on the left) and Gladstone Avenue (right). One of the terracotta-fronted shops on the right has now been turned into a mosque.

High Street North, *c.* 1905. Note the tram lines; East Ham opened its electric tramway service in 1901. Wordsworth Road is on the left, Kensington Avenue on the right. The furnishing stores, No. 272, is now a Hindu temple.

High Street North, *c.* 1910. East Ham Post Office stands on the extreme left, on the corner of Wakefield Street. Also on the left, Oak Hall can be seen, beyond which is the Premier cinema, opened in 1906 and later becoming the Gaumont. Closing in 1963, it became a bingo hall.

High Street North, 1903. Tramcar No. 20, newly converted to covered top, makes its way towards East
Ham station (on the left).

High Street North, *c.* 1908. St John's Church can be seen on the left. It was demolished for a Co-op department store in 1925 and the site is now a car park. St John's Road is the only local commemoration.

Romford Road, *c.* 1954. This photograph was taken from outside the Earl of Essex, looking east.

Green Street, *c.* 1905. The northern end of this street was formerly known as Gipsy Lane. Harold Road is on the left with Boots the chemist standing on the corner, as it does to this day.

Katherine Road. Earlier known as Red Post Lane, this street was renamed in honour of Elizabeth Fry's daughter, Katharine. These shops stood between Lawrence Road and Heigham Road.

The old tollgate, Barking Road. Barking Road was constructed across what was then open land in about 1812 from East India Docks to Barking. As a turnpike road it charged a toll and the toll-gate formerly stood close to the present site of the Denmark Arms.

Barking Road, *c.* 1910. By 1910, however, the old toll-gate had been swept away and parades of shops erected on both sides. Both East Ham Town Hall and the Methodist Central Hall can be seen on the right.

Barking Road, *c.* 1905. A slightly earlier view – Central Hall, built in 1906, is not shown.

Montpelier Gardens, *c.* 1925. This street is typical of the large Central Park estate, solid suburban houses for the upper working class and lower middle class, such as clerks and skilled journeymen.

Chestnut Avenue, Forest Gate, *c.* 1910. This part of Forest Gate, known as the Hamfrith estate, was developed from 1872 onwards and the quiet tree-lined streets of larger houses were intended to attract well-to-do people.

Plashet Grove. Plashet Library, opened in 1899, can be seen on the left, while tram car No. 13 trundles towards the High Street. This area was developed piecemeal for housing in the 1890s.

Manor Park. A multi-card offering views of Manor Park, a name which gradually came to replace that of Little Ilford. The area was built up in the 1880s and 1890s and while much of the housing is still standing and of good quality, some of the terraces built close to the Roding were jerry-built and subject to flooding.

Little Ilford Lane. This photograph taken during the 1890s shows how long the rural aspect survived, even in a rapidly-developing area like Manor Park. The view shows the road (which still curves at this point) opposite where Little Ilford School now stands.

Savage Gardens, *c.* 1904. This Beckton estate was opened in 1903 to provide good quality municipal maisonettes for working-class families.

Savage Gardens, *c.* 1965. The same street half a century later. Beddall's Farm – the last working farm in East Ham – stood behind this road, lending a rural air to the estate and indeed the whole area was jokingly known to locals as Nanny Goat Island.

Savage Gardens, *c.* 1975. A decade later the estate had deteriorated and is seen here boarded up and ready for demolition.

Savage Gardens, *c.* 1985. The London Docklands Development Corporation (LDDC) was established in 1981 to regenerate the area and almost their first act was to redevelop Beckton. New houses, including these striking flats, were built along Savage Gardens in 1982/83.

Winsor Terrace, *c.* 1960. This long terrace was built in about 1870 close to Beckton Gasworks by the Gas Light & Coke Company to house employees. Foremen lived in the larger houses. Named after the company's founder, Winsor Terrace is virtually the only original housing in Beckton to survive the many recent changes in the area.

Mid Beckton, *c*. 1987. After the development of the Beckton Park estate the LDDC developed Mid Beckton in the mid-1980s. Styles had moved on from the 'new town job-lot' styles of Cyprus and an eclectic architectural mix was offered, ranging from 'traditional Essex' (a bit of weatherboarding) to the 'Victorian London square' seen here in Greenwich Crescent.

North Beckton, *c*. 1987. The north side of Tollgate Road was developed towards the end of the 1980s. Here architectural imagination was left to run riot and a variety of odd styles was the result, as seen here in these stock brick houses with distinctive lunette windows.

Renfrew Close, New Beckton *c.* 1985. The former New Beckton estate had also been rebuilt along modern lines by Newham Council.

West Beckton. Custom House, strictly speaking in West Ham rather than East Ham, had been dominated since 1928 by West Ham Stadium, at first used for speedway racing and later for greyhound racing. In this aerial view Prince Regent Lane can be seen to the right of the stadium, stretching down to the docks.

Stadium estate, West Beckton. Following the closure of the stadium in 1972 and its demolition the following year, the area was redeveloped for housing in a joint Greater London Council/Newham Council initiative. The roads built were named after West Ham speedway stars; Young Road seen here commemorates Jack Young.

Atkinson Road. This street commemorates Arthur Atkinson, another West Ham speedway star.

SECTION TWELVE

TRANSPORT

East Ham station. Opened by the London Tilbury & Southend Railway in 1858; for half a century it was a relatively rural halt, as can be seen from this photograph of 1893. A weekly cattle market was held behind the station until the turn of the century.

North Woolwich station. The Eastern Counties Railway opened its branch line to North Woolwich in 1847. The arrival of the railway spurred on the growth of riverside industry and, more importantly, the construction of the Royal Docks. This was precisely as intended by the railway's promoter, the entrepreneur George Parker Bidder. This station, built in 1854, has since become the North Woolwich Old Station Museum with a new station building opened in 1979.

LT & SR Locomotive No.15 *East Ham*. The London Tilbury & Southend Railway, which opened in 1854, at first extended only as far as Tilbury, but by 1856 it had arrived at Southend. The locomotives serving the route were all named after stations on the line. This is No. 15, *East Ham*, a sturdy 4-4-2 tank engine built in 1881 by Sharp Stewart and scrapped in 1932.

Royal Albert Dock Railway. When the Royal Albert Dock was opened in 1880, the dock company began operating its own private railway within the dock area. The line ran from Custom House to the terminus at Gallions Hotel. From 1896 the Great Eastern Railway took over the working. This photograph shows RADR Locomotive No. 6, a 2-4-0 Allan type with external cylinders.

Royal Albert Dock Railway, Locomotive No. 7.

The Gallions Line. PLA locomotive No. 70 seen here with an LMS carriage set on its way to Gallions. The line closed on 7 September 1940.

Gallions station. RADR Locomotive No. 7 seen here at Gallions station bound for Custom House.

Beckton Railway. When Beckton Gasworks was opened in 1870 it incorporated an integrated railway system connected to the rest of the network via a line across East Ham Level to Custom House. This line brought workmen to the plant until the closure of passenger services in 1940. This view shows part of the high-level trackway which connected the various retort houses.

Beckton Railway locomotive. The gasworks railway had its own locomotives and rolling stock, with 42 miles of track. This rare photograph shows No.1, built in 1870, an 0-4-0 tank. A few of these engines are still running on preserved railways, but the Beckton Railway itself closed down in 1970.

Manor Park station, 1891. The Eastern Counties (later Great Eastern) Railway opened a line from London to Romford in 1839 which reached Colchester by 1843, with a further line opened to Southend in 1889. Manor Park station was opened in 1872 and rebuilt in 1893–4. This view shows the old station in the grip of the 'Great Frost' which characterized the winter of 1890–91.

Barking to Beckton tram. Barking Council opened a tramway from Barking Town to Beckton Gasworks in 1903. This Beckton-bound tram waits at the Barking terminus.

Beckton Tramway bascule bridge. To run the new tramway a bridge had to be built across the Roding which would allow shipping continued access to Barking Town Quay. This curious bascule bridge was the result. With the advent of a motor bus service in 1929 both tramway and bridge ceased operations.

The Woolwich Ferry. There has been a ferry crossing between Woolwich and North Woolwich since time immemorial, but the start of the modern service can be dated to 1847 when the railway to North Woolwich opened. Two paddle-boats plied the route, for which there was a toll. In 1889, however, London County Council inaugurated a free ferry service which is still in existence today.

The *Duncan*. The railway ferry struggled on until 1908, but could not compete with the free service offered by the *Duncan*, the *Hutton* and the *Gordon*, the first LCC ferries, each weighing 490 tonnes and able to carry 1,000 passengers and fifteen to twenty vehicles.

The *John Benn*. By 1930 the earlier vessels like the *Duncan* had been supplemented by two larger boats, the *Will Crooks* and the *John Benn*, each displacing 625 tonnes.

The *John Burns*. In 1963 the old paddle steamers were withdrawn, replaced by three diesel vessels each displacing 738 tonnes. The *John Burns* was named after the leader of the 1889 dockers' strike.

SECTION THIRTEEN

WAR

Women workers at Beckton Gasworks. During the First World War women took over almost all the jobs in Beckton Gasworks, including charging and cleaning the retorts (seen here), once thought to be too physically demanding for women.

East Ham war memorial. In the First World War 1,600 East Ham men died. Their names appear on this striking memorial, completed in 1921 and standing in Central Park.

Plaque in East Ham Memorial Hospital. The hospital was built at a cost of £80,000 which was raised entirely by public subscription as a permanent memorial to East Ham's war dead. This plaque in the entrance hall commemorated their sacrifice.

Bombers over East Ham. The industrial and dock areas of East and West Ham were key Luftwaffe targets and suffered badly during the Blitz. This photograph shows bombers over East Ham. The oval of West Ham Stadium can be seen in the centre, while Tollgate Road stretches diagonally across between the two planes. The docks lie to the left.

Beckton Gasworks during the Blitz. The overhead railway has been smashed and wagons hang crazily out of the high level entrance. Compare this scene with that at the top of p. 119.

Beckton Gasworks, showing further Blitz damage.

Firefighting in Beckton Gasworks. Workers on firewatch duty rush to put out a fire in the gasworks. Supplies were interrupted briefly after 'Black Saturday' (7 September 1940), the first day of the Blitz, but despite many direct hits the gasworks continued to operate throughout the war.

VE Day parade. Mayor Wood stands on the steps of East Ham Town Hall flanked by dignitaries and surrounded by allied flags to watch the victory parade.

Prefab houses, Beaconsfield Street. The bombing left East Ham with a serious housing shortage which was partly remedied by the erection of large numbers of prefabricated houses on open land. This view shows Beaconsfield Street, in Cyprus, a veritable prefab city.

Prefab house, Stannard Crescent. The prefab houses were supposed to have a life span of about ten years, but quickly became an established part of the East Ham scene, particularly in Beckton where there was little other housing. This bungalow in Stannard Crescent, Cyprus, survived until 1985.

Beckton in the 'Vietnam War'. Following the closure of Beckton Gasworks, the site was rented out as a filmset and has featured in numerous movies. Here it has been transformed into a Vietnamese city for the Stanley Kubrick film about the Vietnam War, *Full Metal Jacket*.